THE DEBT-FREE BLUEPRINT

THE DEBT-FREE BLUEPRINT

JULES HAWTHORNE

CONTENTS

1	Introduction: The Debt-Free Blueprint	1
2	Chapter 2: Setting Financial Goals	5
3	Chapter 3: Creating a Budget	9
4	Chapter 4: Managing Debt	13
5	Chapter 5: Saving Strategies	17
6	Chapter 6: Investing for the Future	21
7	Chapter 7: Building an Emergency Fund	25
8	Chapter 8: Maximizing Income	29
9	Chapter 9: Minimizing Expenses	33
10	Chapter 10: Developing a Debt Repayment Plan	37
11	Chapter 11: Building Credit	41
12	Chapter 12: Understanding Insurance	45
13	Chapter 13: Estate Planning	49
14	Chapter 14: Tax Planning	53
15	Chapter 15: Retirement Planning	57
16	Chapter 16: Real Estate Investments	61
17	Chapter 17: Stock Market Investments	65

18	Chapter 18: Building a Diversified Portfolio	69
19	Chapter 19: Entrepreneurship and Business Ownershi	73
20	Chapter 20: Passive Income Streams	77
21	Chapter 21: Financial Education and Literacy	81
22	Chapter 22: Mindset and Psychology of Wealth	85
23	Chapter 23: Success Stories and Case Studies	89
24	Chapter 24: Financial Mistakes to Avoid	93
25	Chapter 25: Strategies for Long-Term Wealth Preser	97
26	Chapter 26: Philanthropy and Giving Back	101
27	Chapter 27: Financial Independence and Early Retir	105
28	Chapter 28: Financial Planning for Different Life	109
29	Chapter 29: Navigating Economic Challenges	113
30	Chapter 30: Balancing Work and Life	117
31	Chapter 31: Resources and Tools	121
32	Chapter 32: Conclusion	125

Copyright © 2024 by Jules Hawthorne
All rights reserved. No part of this book may be reproduced in any manner whatsoever without written permission except in the case of brief quotations embodied in critical articles and reviews.
First Printing, 2024

CHAPTER 1

Introduction: The Debt-Free Blueprint

Welcome to *The Debt-Free Blueprint: Strategies to Build Wealth*. This book is designed to guide you through a transformative journey towards financial freedom. Debt, whether perceived as "good" or "bad," has a creeping nature that can slowly erode financial stability and peace of mind. This blueprint will provide a comprehensive understanding of debt, explore its multifaceted impacts on our lives, and outline a robust plan to eliminate it.

Understanding Debt: Beyond Good and Bad

In our society, debt is often seen in black-and-white terms. There is "good debt," often associated with investments that appreciate over time, such as a mortgage or student loans. Then, there's "bad debt," typically linked to high-interest consumer credit such as credit cards. However, this binary perspective oversimplifies a complex issue. Debt, regardless of its type, can accumulate silently, becoming a significant burden. This book will delve into the nuanced nature of debt, helping you understand its true cost and how it can subtly influence your financial decisions and overall well-being.

The Personal Path to Debt Elimination

Getting out of debt is not a one-size-fits-all journey. This blueprint offers a personalized and concrete plan tailored to your unique circumstances. It will empower you to transform the habits that led to debt accumulation and provide you with the tools to take control of your financial future. Through practical strategies and actionable steps, you will learn to prioritize your spending, establish a disciplined approach to managing money, and create a sustainable path towards debt-free living.

Building True Wealth

Financial freedom is not just about eliminating debt; it's about building true wealth. Wealth that is not defined by the absence of payments but by the presence of financial security and freedom. This book will teach you how to cultivate discipline and prioritize financial goals, enabling you to experience a level of wealth that goes beyond monetary value. You will discover the satisfaction of living without the constant pressure of debt and the joy of making financial decisions based on your values and long-term objectives.

Drawing from Experience

In writing this book, I have drawn on over twenty years of experience in consumer credit and lending. My journey has been shaped by countless lessons learned from overseeing thousands of successful debt repayment plans and professional credit counseling sessions. The principles outlined in this blueprint have stood the test of time and have helped countless individuals achieve financial freedom.

Your Journey Begins Now

As you embark on this journey, remember that success is within your reach. The path to financial freedom requires dedication and effort, but the rewards are immeasurable. Ask yourself, "How bad do I want it?" Your commitment to this journey will determine your success. Thousands of individuals have transformed their lives through these principles, and now it's your turn. Embrace the challenge, trust the process, and take the first step towards a debt-free and prosperous future.

CHAPTER 2

Chapter 2: Setting Financial Goals

Setting financial goals is a crucial step towards achieving financial freedom. By creating a well-structured plan of action, you can transform your financial dreams into achievable milestones. This chapter will guide you through the process of defining your financial goals, creating actionable plans, and staying on track to reach them.

Creating a Plan of Action

Achieving financial goals begins with a clear and actionable plan. Here's how to get started:

1. **Set a Target Date for Each Goal**: Determine when you want to achieve each of your financial goals. Having a specific timeline provides a sense of urgency and helps you stay focused.
2. **Calculate the Amount Needed**: Estimate the amount of money required to reach each goal by the target date. While predicting future rates of inflation or investment returns is challenging, you can use financial planning forms to approximate the future value of your lump sum.

3. **Future Value of Lump Sum**: This calculation helps you understand how much a single investment made today will grow over time. It's a fundamental step in long-term financial planning, ensuring you have the necessary funds when you need them.
4. **Regular Investments**: To reach a future monetary target, determine how much you need to invest regularly. A longer timeline generally means smaller monthly investments, making the goal more attainable.
5. **Plan for the Worst**: While investments offer the best-case scenario, it's wise to prepare for financial emergencies. Calculate how long it would take to accomplish your goal if you could only make minimum monthly investments during tough times.
6. **Realistic Goal Assessment**: Compare the number from your future value calculation to the time needed to reach the goal. Assess whether the goal is realistic given your current financial situation. If it seems too strenuous or requires drastic changes, reconsider and adjust your goals accordingly.

Defining Financial Goals

Clear financial goals provide direction and purpose for your financial journey. Here's how to define and prioritize them:

1. **Short-Term Goals**: These are expenses or purchases you plan to make in the near future, typically within a year or less. Examples include building an emergency fund, saving for a vacation, or paying off a small debt. Short-term goals help you manage immediate financial needs and establish good financial habits.

2. **Long-Term Goals**: These are significant financial objectives that take several years to achieve, such as saving for retirement, buying a home, or funding your children's education. Long-term goals should drive your financial decisions and shape your overall strategy.
3. **List Your Goals**: Write down at least three short-term and three long-term goals. Clearly defining these goals will help you make informed decisions and stay motivated.

Balancing Debt Repayment and Savings

A common dilemma is deciding whether to save money or pay off debt first. Here's a balanced approach:

1. **Assess Your Financial Situation**: Review your income, expenses, and debt. Understand your financial landscape to make informed choices.
2. **Prioritize High-Interest Debt**: Paying off high-interest debt, such as credit card balances, should be a priority. High-interest payments can significantly impede your financial progress.
3. **Build an Emergency Fund**: Simultaneously, work on building an emergency fund. Aim for at least three to six months' worth of living expenses to cover unexpected events without relying on debt.
4. **Allocate Funds Wisely**: Once you have a plan for high-interest debt and an emergency fund, allocate funds towards your savings and investments. Balance your approach to ensure steady progress towards both debt reduction and wealth building.

CHAPTER 3

Chapter 3: Creating a Budget

Creating a budget is a pivotal step in achieving financial stability and freedom. It's the foundation upon which you can build your financial future. While it might seem tedious or unexciting, budgeting is the only way to truly gain control over your finances. This chapter will guide you through the process of creating a practical and effective budget.

Step 1: Determine Your Total Monthly Income

The first step in creating a budget is to figure out your total monthly income. This includes all sources of income:

- **Paychecks**: Include your regular salary or wages.
- **Child Support**: Count any child support payments you receive.
- **Other Sources**: Consider additional income such as side gigs, freelance work, rental income, or any other regular money inflows.

If your income varies, as is often the case with sales jobs or freelance work, it's wise to base your budget on the lowest income amount you've received in recent months. This conservative approach ensures that you can cover your expenses even during less prosperous periods.

Step 2: Calculate Your Monthly Expenses

Next, add up all your monthly bills and living expenses. This typically includes:

- **Housing**: Rent or mortgage payments, property taxes, and homeowner's insurance.
- **Utilities**: Electricity, water, gas, internet, and phone bills.
- **Transportation**: Car payments, insurance, fuel, public transportation costs.
- **Groceries and Household Supplies**: Regular shopping for food and essentials.
- **Debt Payments**: Credit card payments, personal loans, student loans.
- **Insurance**: Health, life, and other insurance premiums.
- **Entertainment and Dining Out**: Any discretionary spending on non-essentials.
- **Savings and Investments**: Contributions to savings accounts, retirement funds, and other investments.

Step 3: Subtract Expenses from Income

Subtract your total monthly expenses from your total monthly income. This will show you how much money you have left each month to allocate towards other expenses or savings. If you find that your expenses exceed your income, it's crucial to identify areas where you can cut back.

Importance of Budgeting

Budgeting is essential for getting out of debt and staying out of debt. It helps you:

- **Gain Control**: Understand exactly where your money is going.
- **Prioritize Spending**: Ensure that your most important expenses are covered.
- **Identify Waste**: Spot and eliminate unnecessary expenditures.
- **Set Financial Goals**: Allocate funds towards achieving your financial objectives.

Family Involvement

Budgeting should be a collective effort, especially if you have a family. Organize a family meeting to discuss your financial goals and set a budget for the month ahead. Open communication ensures everyone is on the same page and committed to the plan. Here are a few tips for effective family budgeting:

- **Transparency**: Share all financial details with your family members.
- **Goal Setting**: Involve everyone in setting short-term and long-term financial goals.
- **Commitment**: Ensure all family members understand the importance of sticking to the budget.
- **Consequences**: Discuss the potential consequences of not adhering to the budget and agree on measures to stay accountable.

Overcoming Common Budgeting Challenges

Many budgets fail because they are not clearly defined or there's a lack of commitment. Here are some strategies to overcome common challenges:

- **Flexibility**: Build some flexibility into your budget to account for unexpected expenses.
- **Review and Adjust**: Regularly review your budget and adjust it as needed to stay on track.
- **Tools and Apps**: Utilize budgeting tools and apps to simplify the process and keep track of your finances.

CHAPTER 4

Chapter 4: Managing Debt

Managing debt is a critical aspect of achieving financial freedom and building wealth. It's essential to understand the different types of debt and how they impact your financial health. This chapter will guide you through the nuances of debt management, helping you distinguish between good and bad debt and providing strategies to effectively manage and leverage debt for your financial benefit.

Understanding Good Debt vs. Bad Debt

Not all debt is created equal. It's important to differentiate between "good" debt and "bad" debt.

1. **Good Debt**: This type of debt is typically low-interest and used to finance investments that generate long-term value. Examples include:
    - **Student Loans**: Investing in education can increase your earning potential over time.
    - **Mortgages**: Real estate generally appreciates in value, making it a worthwhile investment.

- **Business Loans**: Borrowing to start or expand a business can lead to significant returns.
2. **Bad Debt**: High-interest debt that doesn't contribute to long-term financial growth falls into this category. Common examples include:
    - **Credit Cards**: These often carry high-interest rates, making it costly if not paid off monthly.
    - **High-Interest Personal Loans**: Borrowing at high-interest rates for non-essential expenses can lead to financial strain.

The Impact of High-Interest Debt

High-interest debts can significantly hinder your financial progress. If you carry a balance on high-interest credit cards or other expensive loans, you end up paying a substantial amount in interest. This reduces your ability to save and invest, impacting your future wealth.

For example, consider a mortgage of $200,000 with a 5% interest rate, resulting in $10,000 in annual interest payments. If you have an investment returning $10,000 annually, you're essentially breaking even. However, if your debt's interest rate exceeds your investment return, you're effectively losing money each year.

Strategies for Managing Debt

1. **Prioritize High-Interest Debt**: Focus on paying off high-interest debts first. This approach, known as the debt avalanche method, saves you money in the long run by reducing the amount of interest you pay.
2. **Consolidate Debt**: If you have multiple high-interest debts, consider consolidating them into a single, lower-interest loan.

This simplifies your payments and can lower your overall interest rate.
3. **Create a Debt Repayment Plan**: Outline a plan to systematically pay off your debts. Allocate extra money towards the highest-interest debt while making minimum payments on others. Once the highest-interest debt is paid off, move to the next one.
4. **Avoid New Debt**: While paying off existing debt, avoid taking on new debt. This may require lifestyle adjustments and careful budgeting to ensure you live within your means.
5. **Seek Professional Help**: If managing debt feels overwhelming, consider seeking help from a financial advisor or a credit counseling service. They can provide personalized advice and strategies to manage and reduce your debt.

Leveraging Good Debt

While managing and eliminating bad debt is crucial, leveraging good debt can be a strategic move to build wealth. Here's how to use good debt effectively:

1. **Borrow at Low Interest**: Ensure that any debt you take on has a low-interest rate. This minimizes the cost of borrowing and maximizes the potential return on investment.
2. **Tax Advantages**: Certain types of debt, like mortgages and student loans, offer tax benefits. Deductible interest can reduce your taxable income, making borrowing more affordable.
3. **Invest in Appreciating Assets**: Use debt to invest in assets that are likely to appreciate over time, such as real estate or education. The key is to ensure that the returns on these investments outweigh the costs of borrowing.

4. **Responsible Borrowing**: Be prudent with leveraging. Only borrow what you can realistically repay and ensure that the investment justifies the debt.

CHAPTER 5

Chapter 5: Saving Strategies

To start saving money, the key is to begin today. By adopting effective saving strategies, you can build a solid financial foundation and prepare for future goals and emergencies. This chapter will guide you through practical saving techniques that can make a significant difference in your financial journey.

Pay Yourself First

One of the most fundamental principles of saving is to **pay yourself first**. Before paying your living expenses, prioritize setting aside a portion of your income for savings. Aim to put aside at least 10% of your paycheck. If saving this amount isn't feasible, start with a smaller percentage and gradually increase it as you adjust your budget.

Create a Realistic Budget

A realistic budget is essential to ensure you can save consistently. Here's how to get started:

1. **Track Your Income and Expenses**: Document all sources of income and your monthly expenses. Understanding your cash flow will help you identify areas where you can cut back.

2. **Identify Savings Opportunities**: Look for ways to reduce spending in non-essential areas. This could include dining out less, canceling unused subscriptions, or finding more affordable alternatives for regular expenses.
3. **Allocate Savings**: Once you've identified potential savings, allocate these funds to your savings account as soon as you receive your paycheck. This reduces the temptation to spend the money on non-essential items.

Automated Savings

Automated savings can help you save consistently without having to think about it. Here are a few methods to consider:

1. **Automatic Transfers**: Set up an automatic transfer from your everyday account to your savings account every payday. For example, transferring $200 each payday ensures regular contributions to your savings.
2. **Round-Up Savings**: Some banks offer round-up programs where every purchase you make with your debit card is rounded up to the nearest dollar, and the difference is transferred to your savings account. Over time, these small amounts can add up significantly.

Set Clear Savings Goals

Setting specific savings goals can help maintain your motivation and provide a benchmark for progress. Here's how to set effective goals:

1. **Emergency Fund**: Your first goal should be to establish an emergency fund. Aim for at least $1,000 initially, and gradu-

ally increase it to cover three to six months' worth of living expenses.
2. **Specific Targets**: Define what you're saving for, such as a vacation, a new car, or a down payment on a house. Clear targets make it easier to stay focused and disciplined.
3. **Track Your Progress**: Regularly review your savings progress and adjust your strategies as needed to stay on track.

Evaluate Your Spending

To maximize your savings, it's crucial to scrutinize your spending habits. Always ask yourself if a purchase is truly necessary. This simple question can help reduce unnecessary expenditures and keep you focused on your financial goals.

Distinguish Between Price and Value

When shopping, it's important to distinguish between the price and the value of an item. Here's how to apply this principle:

1. **Consider Full Price**: Before buying something on sale, ask yourself if you would still purchase it at full price. If the answer is no, reconsider whether you actually need the item.
2. **Evaluate Quality**: Sometimes, paying a higher price for a quality item can be more economical in the long run than constantly replacing cheaper, lower-quality items.

Consistency is Key

Consistency is the cornerstone of successful saving. By developing good financial habits and sticking to your saving strategies, you can steadily build your savings and achieve your financial goals.

CHAPTER 6

Chapter 6: Investing for the Future

Investing is a crucial component of building wealth and ensuring financial security, especially as you plan for retirement. This chapter will guide you through the essential steps for investing, tailored to different stages of life. We'll explore strategies for those nearing retirement, as well as younger workers looking to capitalize on long-term market gains.

Steps for Nearing Retirement

If you're planning to retire in the near future, it's important to take specific steps to secure your financial future:

1. **Review Retirement Accounts**: Assess your 401(k), IRAs, and other retirement accounts. Ensure you're maximizing contributions and taking advantage of any employer matching programs.
2. **Diversify Investments**: As retirement approaches, consider shifting to a more conservative investment mix. Diversifying your portfolio can help protect your savings from market volatility.

3. **Evaluate Income Needs**: Estimate your income needs during retirement. This includes regular expenses, healthcare costs, and leisure activities. Ensure your investments and savings can sustain your lifestyle.
4. **Plan Withdrawals**: Develop a strategy for withdrawing funds from your retirement accounts. Aim to minimize taxes and ensure your money lasts throughout your retirement.

Investing for Younger Workers

For younger workers, investing is a powerful tool to build wealth over time. The stock market, with its historically high returns, is a viable option for long-term growth. Here's a look at the potential impact of starting early:

1. **Start Early**: The earlier you start investing, the more you benefit from compound interest. Consider a hypothetical example:
   - **Hypothetical Example**: An 18-year-old invests $6,000 annually for nine years, then stops investing entirely. By age 65, with an 8% return on investment (ROI), this individual could have $377,000 due to compound interest. The initial $54,000 investment grows significantly over time.
2. **Compound Interest**: Compound interest is a powerful tool that provides substantial growth over the long term. In our example, the $54,000 invested grows to $377,000 due to the accumulation of interest over time. This emphasizes the importance of starting early and letting your investments grow.

Historical Investment Returns

Understanding historical returns can help guide your investment decisions. Here's a look at some historical averages:

- **US Savings Bonds**: On average, US savings bonds returned 7.4% annually between 1926 and 2003.
- **Corporate Bonds**: These typically average a 6% annual return.
- **Stocks**: Historically, stocks have averaged around an 11% annual return.

While past performance does not guarantee future results, historical data can provide a reasonable expectation of potential returns.

Allocating Resources and Leverage

When choosing investments, it's critical to allocate resources wisely:

1. **Compare Investments**: If a stock is expected to return more than a savings bond, it might be wise to invest in the stock, especially if borrowing costs are low.
2. **Use Leverage Carefully**: Leveraging involves borrowing money to invest, with the goal of magnifying returns. For example, using a mortgage to buy a house can be a strategic move if the property's value appreciates. However, leverage comes with risks, as your assets act as collateral. If the investment fails, you could lose your collateral, such as your home.

Risk and Young Investors

Younger investors can typically afford to take on more risk because they have time to recover from potential losses:

1. **High-Risk, High-Return Investments**: Investing in high-risk, high-return stocks can be a viable strategy for young workers. Even if a high-risk investment doesn't pay off, there's still ample time to rebuild and recover.
2. **Diversification**: To manage risk, diversify your investments across different asset classes and sectors. This helps mitigate the impact of any single investment's poor performance.

This chapter aims to equip you with the knowledge and strategies to invest effectively for the future.

CHAPTER 7

Chapter 7: Building an Emergency Fund

Creating an emergency fund is a crucial step in achieving financial stability and preparing for unexpected expenses. An emergency fund acts as a financial safety net, helping you avoid relying on credit cards or loans during tough times. This chapter will guide you through the process of building and maintaining a robust emergency fund.

Start with Automatic Transfers

To build your emergency fund, start by setting up automatic monthly transfers from your checking account to your savings account. This makes saving a regular and effortless part of your financial routine. Here's how to get started:

1. **Determine the Amount**: Decide how much you can afford to save each month, considering your current expenses and financial goals. Even a small amount, saved consistently, can grow significantly over time.
2. **Set Up Transfers**: Arrange for automatic transfers to ensure the money is moved to your savings account without you hav-

ing to think about it. This reduces the temptation to spend the money on non-essential items.

Find Extra Money in Your Budget

Identifying extra money in your budget can accelerate the growth of your emergency fund. Here are some strategies:

1. **Comparison Shopping**: Look for the best quality at the lowest price for every product and service you use. This can free up extra cash to put into savings.
2. **Track Spending**: Keep track of every cent you spend and create a written spending plan. This helps identify areas where you can cut back and save more.
3. **Monthly Leftovers**: At the end of each month, transfer any remaining money in your checking account to your emergency fund. These small amounts can add up over time.

Gradual Increases and Windfalls

To reach your savings goal faster, gradually increase the amount of your automatic transfers over time. Additionally, any extra money you receive, such as bonuses or gifts, should be added to your emergency fund. Here's why:

1. **Avoid Lifestyle Inflation**: Depositing extra money into your savings before you have the chance to spend it prevents lifestyle inflation and unnecessary spending.
2. **Boost Savings Quickly**: Windfalls can provide a significant boost to your emergency fund, helping you reach your goal sooner.

The Importance of an Emergency Fund

Having an emergency fund can save you from financial stress and the costly mistake of using credit cards in emergencies. Here's why it's essential:

1. **Avoid Credit Card Debt**: Using a credit card for emergencies can lead to high-interest debt that takes a long time to pay off.
2. **Financial Security**: An emergency fund provides peace of mind, knowing you can cover unexpected expenses without going into debt.

What Constitutes an Emergency?

Understanding what constitutes an emergency helps ensure your fund is used appropriately. Examples include:

1. **Unexpected Travel**: Needing to fly out of town on short notice for a family emergency.
2. **Urgent Repairs**: Fixing a damaged car or replacing a broken computer.
3. **Medical Expenses**: Covering unexpected medical bills.

Emergencies often come in waves, so having a well-funded emergency account means you won't still be paying off past emergencies when new ones arise. Aim to cover at least three to six months' worth of living expenses with your emergency fund.

Staying Committed to Your Fund

Building and maintaining an emergency fund requires commitment and discipline. Here are some tips to stay on track:

1. **Regular Reviews**: Periodically review your savings goals and adjust your budget as needed.

2. **Celebrate Milestones**: Celebrate reaching savings milestones to stay motivated.
3. **Stay Disciplined**: Avoid dipping into your emergency fund for non-emergencies to ensure it's available when truly needed.

This chapter aims to equip you with practical strategies to build a solid emergency fund.

CHAPTER 8

Chapter 8: Maximizing Income

Increasing your income can significantly impact your ability to pay off debt and build wealth. By exploring various strategies, you can find ways to enhance your earnings and secure your financial future. This chapter will provide insights into different avenues for boosting your income, from asking for a raise or promotion to starting a side business.

Working Hard and Making Sacrifices

In general, the key to getting a raise or promotion is demonstrating your value to your employer. This often involves working hard and making sacrifices, such as:

1. **Unpaid Overtime**: Volunteering for extra hours without additional pay shows dedication and commitment to your job.
2. **Additional Qualifications**: Pursuing relevant certifications or advanced degrees can make you more valuable to your employer.
3. **Taking Work Home**: Completing tasks outside of regular working hours can demonstrate your willingness to go above and beyond.

Proving Your Worth

To effectively argue for increased pay, you need to prove that you are worth the additional investment. This can involve:

1. **Documenting Achievements**: Keep a record of your accomplishments and contributions to the company. Highlight how your work has positively impacted the organization.
2. **Performance Reviews**: Use performance reviews to gather positive feedback from supervisors and colleagues. This evidence can support your case for a raise or promotion.
3. **Benchmarking Salaries**: Research industry standards for your position to ensure you are being compensated fairly. Presenting this information can strengthen your argument.

Lucky Breaks

Sometimes, you may be offered a pay increase or promotion without asking for it. This can happen if:

1. **Recognition**: Your employer recognizes and rewards your hard work.
2. **Retention**: Your employer wants to keep you from accepting a potential job offer from another company.

Asking for a Raise or Promotion

When asking for a raise or promotion, preparation and timing are crucial. Here's how to approach the conversation:

1. **Prepare Your Case**: Gather evidence of your achievements and contributions. Be ready to explain how you've added value to the company.

2. **Choose the Right Time**: Timing is key. Request a meeting during a period of company growth or after a successful project.
3. **Practice Your Pitch**: Rehearse what you will say. Be confident but not arrogant. Clearly state your request and back it up with facts.

Exploring Additional Income Streams

Beyond asking for a raise or promotion, there are numerous ways to increase your income. Here are a few ideas to consider:

1. **Starting a Side Business**: Identify a skill or passion that can be monetized. This could be anything from freelance writing to selling handmade crafts online.
2. **Gig Economy Jobs**: Consider part-time work in the gig economy, such as driving for a ride-sharing service, delivering food, or performing freelance tasks.
3. **Investing**: If you have some capital, explore investment opportunities. This could include stocks, real estate, or other investment vehicles.
4. **Rental Income**: If you have extra space, consider renting out a room or property. Platforms like Airbnb can help you generate additional income.
5. **Skill Development**: Continuously improve your skills through online courses or workshops. Higher skill levels can lead to better-paying job opportunities.

Planting the Seeds of Thought

The purpose of this chapter is to plant the seeds of thought about potential ways to increase your income. While we can't cover every possible method, the key is to stay open-minded and proactive.

Explore different avenues, evaluate their feasibility, and take action on those that align with your skills and interests.

This chapter aims to provide you with ideas and options to maximize your income.

CHAPTER 9

Chapter 9: Minimizing Expenses

Being overburdened by debt and expenses is a common problem, but many people find themselves ill-equipped to accurately track their daily expenditures. This can lead to feelings of helplessness and unnecessary stress. However, the advent of internet banking provides a convenient and painless method to track your finances and learn where your money is actually going. By effectively managing your expenses, you can gain control of your financial situation and build long-term wealth.

Leveraging Internet Banking

Internet banking has revolutionized the way we manage our finances. Most major banks offer facilities to automatically categorize and chart your income and expenditures. Here's how to make the most of these tools:

1. **Automatic Categorization**: Banks can automatically sort your transactions into categories such as groceries, utilities, and entertainment. This helps you see where your money is going at a glance.

2. **Charts and Graphs**: Visual representations like pie charts and bar graphs provide a clear overall picture of your financial situation. For example, a pie graph showing "expenses as a percentage of income" can reveal if too much income is being devoted to credit card repayments or other specific expenses.
3. **Identifying Problem Areas**: Recognizing areas where you are overspending is key to finding ways to cut costs. This data can help you increase the efficiency of your expenditures and build long-term wealth.

Understanding the Psychology of Consumption

Everyone prioritizes different things in their lives and allocates a portion of their income accordingly. Whether it's a particular brand of shoes, a car, or a smoking habit, we are all influenced by the psychology of consumption. Here's how to manage it:

1. **Identify Less Important Expenses**: Determine what is less important to you in relative terms. The money saved by downgrading or cutting out these expenses can be redirected towards more significant financial goals, such as paying off your mortgage or building an emergency fund.
2. **Make Conscious Choices**: Evaluate your current expenditure and ask yourself, "What can I get rid of?" This could involve downgrading services, cutting unnecessary subscriptions, or eliminating habits that drain your finances.

Practical Steps to Minimize Expenses

Here are some practical steps to help you minimize your expenses and maximize savings:

1. **Review Subscriptions**: Are you using your gym membership as often as you should? Could you handle a downgrade in your cable or streaming services? Cancel or reduce subscriptions that you don't fully utilize.
2. **Evaluate Daily Habits**: Do you need bottled water, or would tap water suffice? If you are a smoker or enjoy alcoholic beverages, consider reducing or eliminating these habits. The savings can add up quickly.
3. **Comparison Shopping**: Look for the best deals on products and services. Comparison shopping ensures you get the best quality at the lowest price, freeing up extra cash for savings or investments.
4. **Create a Spending Plan**: Track every cent you spend and create a written spending plan. This helps you stay within your budget and identify areas where you can cut back.
5. **Automate Savings**: Set up automatic transfers to your savings account. Any remaining money left in your checking account at the end of the month can be added to your savings or investment accounts.

Reducing Lifestyle Inflation

Lifestyle inflation occurs when your spending increases as your income rises. Avoid this by making mindful choices about your spending:

1. **Avoid Upgrading Too Soon**: Just because you get a raise doesn't mean you need to upgrade your car or move to a more expensive apartment. Stick to your current lifestyle and direct the extra income towards savings or debt repayment.

2. **Stay Focused on Goals**: Keep your long-term financial goals in mind. Redirecting surplus income towards these goals can help you achieve financial freedom sooner.

By carefully managing your expenses and making conscious choices about your spending, you can reduce unnecessary costs and build a solid foundation for long-term financial success.

This chapter aims to provide you with practical strategies to minimize expenses and gain control over your finances.

CHAPTER 10

Chapter 10: Developing a Debt Repayment Plan

If you're reading this, it means you're ready to turn your financial situation around. Many people find themselves burdened by debt without a clear plan to get out. Developing a debt repayment plan is essential for achieving financial freedom. This chapter will guide you through the steps to create an effective strategy for paying off your debts.

Assessing Your Debt

The first step in developing a debt repayment plan is to assess your current debt situation. You need to answer the following questions:

1. **How much do I owe?**: Make a list of all your debts, including credit cards, loans, and any other outstanding balances.
2. **What are the interest rates on my debts?**: Identify the interest rates for each debt. This will help you prioritize which debts to pay off first.
3. **What are the minimum payments on each debt?**: Determine the minimum monthly payments required for each debt.

4. **How much can I realistically pay off each month?**: Evaluate your budget to see how much you can afford to allocate towards debt repayment each month.

Prioritizing Your Debts

To effectively pay off your debts, prioritize them based on interest rates and balances. Here are two common methods:

1. **Debt Avalanche Method**: Focus on paying off the debt with the highest interest rate first while making minimum payments on other debts. Once the highest-interest debt is paid off, move to the next highest, and so on. This method saves you the most money on interest in the long run.
2. **Debt Snowball Method**: Focus on paying off the smallest debt first while making minimum payments on others. Once the smallest debt is paid off, move to the next smallest, and so on. This method provides quick wins and can boost your motivation.

Creating a Debt Repayment Plan

A debt repayment plan is a roadmap to becoming debt-free. Here's how to create one:

1. **List Your Debts**: Start by listing all your debts, including the creditor, balance, interest rate, and minimum payment.
2. **Set a Timeline**: Determine a realistic timeline for paying off each debt. This can help you stay on track and measure your progress.
3. **Allocate Payments**: Allocate as much money as possible towards the highest-priority debt while making minimum pay-

ments on others. As each debt is paid off, redirect the freed-up funds to the next priority debt.
4. **Minimize Living Expenses**: Reduce your living expenses to free up more money for debt repayment. This may involve cutting back on non-essential spending or finding ways to lower your monthly bills.

Staying Committed

Staying committed to your debt repayment plan requires dedication and discipline. Here are some tips to help you stay on track:

1. **Track Your Progress**: Regularly review your debts and track your progress. Seeing the balances decrease can be motivating.
2. **Celebrate Milestones**: Celebrate when you pay off a debt or reach a significant milestone. Rewarding yourself in small, meaningful ways can keep you motivated.
3. **Adjust as Needed**: Life happens, and sometimes you may need to adjust your plan. If unexpected expenses arise, don't get discouraged. Adjust your plan and keep moving forward.

Learning from Past Mistakes

Understanding how you got into debt in the first place is crucial to avoid repeating the same mistakes. Reflect on your spending habits and financial decisions. For instance, Drew's story illustrates how uncontrolled spending led to debt. By recognizing the consequences of past actions, you can make more informed decisions moving forward.

The Importance of Sacrifice

Achieving debt freedom often requires making sacrifices. It may mean living on a tighter budget temporarily, but the long-term benefits are worth it. By putting your debts first, you can accelerate your journey to financial freedom.

CHAPTER 11

Chapter 11: Building Credit

Building credit is an essential aspect of managing your financial health and gaining access to favorable borrowing terms. Understanding the nuances of credit and how to effectively build it can save you money and provide financial flexibility. This chapter will guide you through strategies for building and maintaining good credit.

Understanding Types of Loans and Upfront Fees

When taking out loans, be mindful of upfront borrowing fees. Sometimes, it may be beneficial to borrow slightly more than you need and invest the excess amount safely in case the need arises again. Here are a few key points to consider:

1. **Mortgages**: Mortgages typically carry the lowest possible interest rates because the home acts as collateral. This reduces the lender's risk and can make it an attractive option for long-term borrowing.
2. **Installment Loans**: Installment loans, such as car loans or education loans, carry fixed rates and are repaid over a set period. By making consistent payments, you demonstrate reliability to lenders, which can improve your credit score.

Credit Cards and High-Interest Loans

Credit cards are essentially high-interest loans. While using a credit card and paying it off immediately can build credit, it's not always the most effective method. Here's why:

1. **High Interest Rates**: Credit cards often come with high interest rates, which can be costly if you carry a balance from month to month.
2. **Building Credit with Installment Loans**: A more effective way to build credit is through installment loans with fixed rates. Start with loans that have the lowest rates available, such as car loans or student loans. By making regular payments, you demonstrate your reliability as a borrower, which can enhance your credit profile.

Avoiding Debt to Build Credit

Contrary to popular belief, you don't need to incur debt to build credit. Here's why:

1. **Responsible Credit Use**: High school and college students are often advised to get credit cards to build credit. However, this can lead to financial trouble if not managed responsibly. It's important to use credit wisely and avoid accumulating unnecessary debt.
2. **Alternative Methods**: Other ways to build credit include paying off small loans or using secured credit cards, which require a cash deposit that serves as your credit limit.

Key Components of a Credit Score

Understanding how the credit system works is crucial for building and maintaining good credit. Here are the key components:

1. **Payment History**: Your payment history is the most significant factor in your credit score. Make all payments on time to establish a positive track record.
2. **Credit Utilization**: This refers to the amount of credit you're using compared to your credit limit. Aim to keep your credit utilization below 30% to improve your score.
3. **Length of Credit History**: The longer your credit history, the better. Keep older accounts open to maintain a longer credit history.
4. **Credit Mix**: Having a mix of different types of credit (e.g., credit cards, installment loans) can positively impact your score.
5. **New Credit Inquiries**: Applying for too many new credit accounts in a short period can lower your score. Space out credit applications to avoid negative impacts.

Building Credit Responsibly

The goal of building credit should be to secure better borrowing terms for significant purchases like a home or car. Here's how to do it responsibly:

1. **Start Small**: If you're new to credit, start with a small, manageable loan or a secured credit card.
2. **Make Timely Payments**: Always make payments on time to build a positive payment history.
3. **Monitor Your Credit Report**: Regularly check your credit report for errors and discrepancies. Dispute any inaccuracies to ensure your report reflects your true credit history.
4. **Use Credit Wisely**: Avoid maxing out credit cards and try to pay off balances in full each month.

Chapter 12: Understanding Insurance

Insurance is a critical component of financial planning, providing protection against unexpected events that can have significant financial consequences. This chapter will guide you through the various types of insurance, their benefits, and how they work to safeguard your financial well-being.

The Importance of Insurance

Insurance plays a vital role in protecting individuals from the financial impact of unforeseen events. Without insurance, events such as accidents, illnesses, or job loss can destabilize your financial position. By transferring the risk to an insurance company, you ensure that you are better prepared for life's uncertainties.

Types of Beneficial Insurance

There are several types of insurance that are particularly beneficial, including health insurance and income insurance. These types of insurance focus on personal welfare, which is one of the most essential aspects of your life.

1. **Health Insurance**: Health insurance covers hospital, medical, and surgical costs in the event you need treatment. This

can include everything from routine check-ups to major surgeries. Having health insurance ensures that you receive necessary medical care without the burden of excessive medical bills.
2. **Income Insurance**: Income insurance provides a portion of your salary if you are unable to work due to illness or injury. Typically, income insurance covers up to 75% of your salary, allowing you to manage your living expenses while you recover. This type of insurance continues until you are able to resume your normal occupation.

How Insurance Works

When you purchase insurance, you transfer the cost of potential loss to the insurance company in exchange for a fee known as the premium. Here's a closer look at the process:

1. **Premiums**: The amount you pay for your insurance policy. Premiums are typically paid monthly, quarterly, or annually.
2. **Claims**: When an insured event occurs, you file a claim with the insurance company to receive compensation. The insurance company reviews the claim and, if approved, pays out according to the terms of the policy.
3. **Investments**: Insurance companies invest the premiums they collect to generate additional revenue. The returns from these investments are used to pay out claims and cover the company's operating costs. The remainder contributes to the company's profit.

Benefits of Insurance

Insurance offers several key benefits that contribute to financial stability and peace of mind:

1. **Protection Against Financial Loss**: Insurance provides a safety net, covering significant expenses that could otherwise deplete your savings or put you in debt.
2. **Peace of Mind**: Knowing that you are protected against unexpected events allows you to live with less stress and focus on other important aspects of your life.
3. **Financial Planning**: Insurance supports long-term financial planning by ensuring that you are covered for major risks and can allocate your savings and investments more effectively.

Avoiding Financial Disasters

Without insurance, unexpected events can have a devastating impact on your financial health. For example, a car accident without auto insurance can lead to high repair costs and potential liability for damages. Similarly, a serious illness without health insurance can result in overwhelming medical bills. Insurance helps mitigate these risks, ensuring that you can manage unexpected expenses without jeopardizing your financial stability.

Chapter 13: Estate Planning

Estate planning is a vital process that ensures your assets are managed and distributed according to your wishes after your death. It's about leaving a lasting legacy for the people and causes you care most about. This chapter will guide you through the essential tools of estate planning, including trusts, life insurance, and wills.

Trusts

A trust is a legal arrangement in which one person (or an institution, such as a bank or trust company) called a "trustee" holds legal title to property for another person, called a "beneficiary." Trusts can be a useful vehicle for managing and growing your wealth over time or for specific purposes. Here are key points about trusts:

1. **Types of Trusts**:
    - **Inter Vivos Trust**: Created while the trust maker is alive. It allows you to manage and distribute your assets during your lifetime and after your death.
    - **Testamentary Trust**: Created in a will and takes effect when the will is probated after the will maker's death.
2. **Benefits of Trusts**:

- **Wealth Management**: Trusts can help in managing your wealth for a period or a specific purpose, such as funding a grandchild's education.
- **Control and Flexibility**: Trusts offer control over how and when your assets are distributed.
- **Protection**: They can protect your assets from creditors and reduce estate taxes.

Life Insurance

Life insurance is primarily used for income replacement, but it can also be an effective tool for wealth transfer. Here's how life insurance can play a role in your estate plan:

1. **Income Replacement**: Life insurance ensures that your dependents have financial support in the event of your untimely death.
2. **Wealth Transfer**: If your children are grown and you're self-insured against premature death, life insurance can be a simple method to transfer wealth to your beneficiaries. The death benefit can provide a tax-free inheritance.

Wills

A will is the cornerstone of an estate plan. It specifies how you want your property distributed, who will care for your minor children, and other important instructions. Here's what you need to know about wills:

1. **Distribution of Property**: A will outlines how your assets will be distributed to your beneficiaries.
2. **Guardianship**: It allows you to designate a guardian for your minor children.

3. **Management of Children's Finances**: You can provide instructions for managing your children's inheritance.
4. **Funeral Arrangements**: A will can include your wishes for funeral and burial arrangements.
5. **Taking Effect**: A will takes effect upon your death and ensures that your property is transferred to the persons or entities you designate.

Tools for Estate Planning

To create a comprehensive estate plan, consider the following tools and steps:

1. **Power of Attorney**: Designate someone to make financial and legal decisions on your behalf if you become incapacitated.
2. **Healthcare Directive**: Outline your medical treatment preferences and appoint someone to make healthcare decisions for you if you're unable to do so.
3. **Beneficiary Designations**: Ensure your retirement accounts, life insurance policies, and other assets have up-to-date beneficiary designations.
4. **Regular Reviews**: Periodically review and update your estate plan to reflect changes in your life, such as marriage, divorce, the birth of a child, or changes in the law.

Chapter 14: Tax Planning

Tax planning is a critical component of any debt reduction or wealth-building strategy. The negative tax consequences that can arise from debt reduction or elimination make it imperative to include tax planning as part of your financial plan. This chapter will guide you through the essentials of tax planning, especially in the context of managing and eliminating debt.

The Importance of Tax Planning

Debt reduction and elimination can generate significant tax consequences. Understanding and planning for these can save you from unexpected expenses. Here's why tax planning is essential:

1. **Tax Liability**: Tax liability is a debt that does not have a statute of limitations, meaning it must be paid regardless of how long it is avoided. Proper tax planning can prevent the accumulation of unmanageable tax debts.

Settled Debt and Tax Implications

There is some good news when it comes to debt that is settled for less than the principal amount or deemed uncollectable. Here's what you need to know:

1. **Non-Taxable Settlements**: Debt settled for less than the principal amount or deemed uncollectable may not cause a tax liability and is not subject to income tax.
2. **Less Painful Options**: For borrowers with no alternative but to settle a debt or declare bankruptcy, understanding these provisions can make ending a bad financial situation less painful.

Bankruptcy and Tax Consequences

Bankruptcy can lead to partial debt discharge, where some debts are forgiven, and others are not. Here's how this impacts tax liability:

1. **Forgiven Debt as Income**: Any debt forgiven in a debt discharge is considered income and is taxable. This can create a significant tax liability.
2. **Consult an Attorney**: Given the complexity of tax implications in bankruptcy, it's crucial to consult with an attorney before making any decisions.

Debt Settlement and Increased Tax Liability

Debt settlement involves negotiating with creditors to pay off a debt for less than the amount owed. Here's what you need to know about the tax implications:

1. **Settlement as Income**: Any forgiven portion of the debt is considered income and is taxable. The lender will issue a 1099 form to both the borrower and the IRS, stating the amount of the forgiven debt.
2. **Marginal Tax Rates**: The forgiven amount will be taxed at your marginal tax rate. A significant settlement can result in a higher tax liability, but it is still only taxed at marginal rates.

Refinancing and Tax Planning

Refinancing high-interest unsecured debt with low-interest secured debt, such as a 30-year home loan, can be a strategic move. Here's why:

1. **Tax Implications**: The income tax liability from secured debt is often insignificant compared to the interest savings from refinancing. Proper planning can ensure you maximize the benefits and minimize tax liabilities.

High-Profile Situations

There are numerous situations where debt reduction or elimination can create tax liabilities. Here are a few high-profile examples:

1. **Mortgage Forgiveness**: Under certain programs, forgiven mortgage debt may not be taxable if specific conditions are met.
2. **Student Loan Forgiveness**: Certain student loan forgiveness programs may result in taxable income, while others do not. Understanding these distinctions is crucial.
3. **Credit Card Debt Settlement**: As mentioned, settled credit card debt is considered income and must be reported to the IRS.

Tax Planning for Debt Elimination and Wealth Building

Effective tax planning can significantly impact your overall financial health. Here are a few tips:

1. **Consult Professionals**: Work with tax professionals or financial advisors to understand the full implications of your debt reduction strategy.

2. **Stay Informed**: Keep up to date with tax laws and regulations that may affect your situation.
3. **Plan Ahead**: Incorporate tax planning into your overall financial strategy to avoid surprises and ensure a smooth path to debt elimination and wealth building.

CHAPTER 15

Chapter 15: Retirement Planning

Retirement planning is a crucial aspect of personal finance that ensures you have enough resources to live comfortably after you stop working. Unfortunately, many people delay asking themselves the critical question: "Will I have enough money to retire?" This chapter will guide you through the essentials of retirement planning, highlighting common pitfalls and effective strategies.

The Wealthy Barber: A Must-Read for Beginners

A great introductory tool for retirement planning is the book *The Wealthy Barber* by David Chilton. This novel, set in a small-town barber shop, revolves around a young man's quest to secure good financial advice from the town's wealthy barber. The story's climax occurs when the protagonist receives a wealth of financial knowledge during a haircut. This knowledge covers many aspects of personal finance, with a prominent focus on retirement planning. The book is an easy yet entertaining read and serves as an excellent starting point for anyone wanting to learn about personal finance. The insights gained can provide great incentive for further research on retirement planning.

Common Mistakes in Retirement Planning

Even those who actively plan for retirement may find themselves using ineffective saving strategies. Here are some common mistakes:

1. **Relying on Bank Savings Accounts**: People who save for retirement by putting money into a bank savings account are making a big mistake. The interest rates on savings accounts are often lower than the rate of inflation, which means savers are losing buying power over time.
2. **Low-Return Investments**: Investing too much in low-return investments is another common error. With the burden of retirement shifting from employers to employees, it's essential to find more effective investment strategies to ensure a comfortable retirement.

The Importance of Research and Effort

Retirement planning is crucial for personal finance, and it warrants thorough research and effort. But where should one begin this research?

1. **Understanding Retirement**: Retirement means different things to different people. For some, it signifies getting old; for others, it represents a great transition out of the work life or a complete mystery. No matter your perspective, it's essential to plan ahead.
2. **Asking the Right Questions**: Begin by asking, "Will I have enough money to retire?" This simple question can drive your planning and decision-making process.

The Reality of Retirement Planning in America

Many Americans are not adequately prepared for retirement. Here are some troubling statistics:

1. **Lack of Formal Plans**: Over half of all Americans do not have a formal retirement plan in place. Many rely on the hope that Social Security will be sufficient to meet their needs.
2. **Risks of Relying on Social Security**: Relying solely on Social Security is risky and often results in a frugal existence. Given the challenges facing Social Security, it's critical to have a comprehensive retirement plan.

Effective Retirement Planning Strategies

To avoid the common pitfalls and effectively plan for retirement, consider the following strategies:

1. **Diversify Investments**: Instead of relying solely on savings accounts, diversify your investments across different asset classes, such as stocks, bonds, and real estate. This can help you achieve higher returns and mitigate risks.
2. **Regular Contributions**: Make regular contributions to retirement accounts, such as 401(k)s or IRAs. Take advantage of employer matching programs if available.
3. **Monitor and Adjust**: Regularly review your retirement plan and make adjustments as needed. This ensures you stay on track to meet your retirement goals.
4. **Professional Advice**: Consult financial advisors to get personalized advice and create a tailored retirement plan that meets your needs and goals.

CHAPTER 16

Chapter 16: Real Estate Investments

Real estate investment can be a highly lucrative avenue for building wealth, but it requires careful planning, market insight, and a significant capital outlay. This chapter will guide you through the essential steps and considerations for successful real estate investment.

Evaluating Market Demand

Before deciding to buy real estate, it's crucial to evaluate the type of properties currently in demand. Here's how to conduct your research:

1. **Market Analysis**: Read newspapers, browse classified ads, and consult real estate market reports to identify trends. This will help you understand which types of properties are sought after.
2. **Consult Experts**: Reach out to friends or acquaintances who work in property or real estate agencies. Their insider knowledge can provide valuable insights into market demand.
3. **Location, Location, Location**: Properties located near public facilities, scenic areas, or vibrant neighborhoods generally

hold more value due to their accessibility and appeal. Such locations are likely to appreciate in value over time, offering better investment opportunities.

Ambitious Investment with Potential High Returns

Real estate investment is more ambitious compared to conservative investments like bonds or savings accounts, which usually offer lower rates of return. Here's why real estate can be a game-changer:

1. **Higher Returns**: Real estate has the potential to provide far greater results due to appreciation in property value and rental income.
2. **Capital Requirement**: It requires a higher initial capital outlay, but with careful planning and informed decisions, the returns can justify the investment.
3. **Risk and Reward**: Like any investment, real estate comes with risks. However, with good insight and calculation, it can become a significant resource for building wealth and potentially solving debt problems.

Steps to Successful Real Estate Investment

To navigate the complexities of real estate investment, follow these steps:

1. **Set Clear Goals**: Define what you want to achieve with your real estate investment. Are you looking for rental income, long-term appreciation, or a quick flip?
2. **Financial Planning**: Assess your financial situation and determine how much capital you can allocate to real estate investment. Consider obtaining financing options if necessary.

3. **Research and Education**: Educate yourself about the real estate market, including local market conditions, property values, and investment strategies. Attend seminars, read books, and seek advice from experienced investors.
4. **Choose the Right Property**: Select properties that align with your investment goals. Consider factors such as location, property condition, and potential for appreciation or rental income.
5. **Conduct Due Diligence**: Perform thorough inspections and evaluations of the property. Assess its structural integrity, legal status, and any potential issues that could affect its value.
6. **Hire Professionals**: Work with real estate agents, attorneys, and financial advisors to ensure you make informed decisions and navigate legal complexities.
7. **Manage the Property**: If you're investing in rental properties, consider hiring a property management company to handle day-to-day operations, tenant relations, and maintenance.
8. **Monitor and Adapt**: Regularly review your investment's performance and adapt your strategy as needed. Stay informed about market trends and be prepared to make adjustments.

The Benefits of Real Estate Investment

Real estate investment offers several advantages that can contribute to financial success:

1. **Appreciation**: Over time, real estate tends to appreciate in value, providing long-term capital gains.
2. **Rental Income**: Rental properties can generate steady cash flow, contributing to your overall income and helping to cover mortgage payments.

3. **Tax Benefits**: Real estate investors can take advantage of various tax deductions, including mortgage interest, property taxes, and depreciation.
4. **Diversification**: Adding real estate to your investment portfolio diversifies your assets, reducing overall risk.

Chapter 17: Stock Market Investments

Investing in the stock market can be a powerful way to build wealth and achieve long-term financial goals. However, it requires careful planning, an understanding of various investment strategies, and awareness of market dynamics. This chapter will guide you through some key concepts and strategies for successful stock market investing.

Direct Stock Purchase Plans (DRPs)

One way to invest in the stock market is through Direct Stock Purchase Plans (DRPs). These plans allow investors to buy shares of a company's stock directly from the company, often bypassing brokers. Here are some benefits of DRPs:

1. **Fractional Shares**: DRPs allow you to purchase fractional shares, making it easier to invest small amounts of money regularly.
2. **Lower Costs**: DRPs can be cheaper than using a broker because they often have lower fees.

3. **Dividend Reinvestment**: Shareholders can reinvest dividends to buy additional shares, which can compound over time and increase investment returns.

Maximizing After-Tax Returns and Minimizing Costs

The key to successful stock market investing is to maximize after-tax returns while minimizing costs. Here are some strategies:

1. **Index Funds**: An index fund is a type of mutual fund designed to replicate the performance of a market index, such as the S&P 500. Index funds are a good tool for beginning investors because they offer:
    - **Low Costs**: Index funds typically have lower fees compared to actively managed funds.
    - **Diversification**: By investing in an index fund, you gain exposure to a broad range of stocks, which helps spread risk.
    - **Consistent Performance**: Index funds aim to match the performance of the market, providing steady long-term returns.

Long-Term Wealth Building

Stock market investments are a key to long-term wealth building and can continue to benefit you even after retirement. Many retirement plans, such as 401(k)s and IRAs, involve stock investments. Additionally, stock investments can facilitate wealth transfer to heirs or charities.

Market Diversification

Market diversification is a critical safety measure for investors. It involves spreading your investments across various asset classes, industries, and geographic regions to reduce risk. Here's how to diversify effectively:

1. **Asset Classes**: Invest in a mix of stocks, bonds, and cash to balance risk and return.
2. **Industries**: Spread your investments across different sectors, such as technology, healthcare, and consumer goods.
3. **Geographic Regions**: Consider investing in both domestic and international markets to mitigate risks associated with any single country's economy.

Historical Perspective and Market Resilience

Understanding historical market trends can provide valuable insights for investors. Despite short-term volatility, the stock market tends to rise in the long term. Here's a historical perspective:

1. **Stock Market Crash of 1983**: The crash affected global markets, followed by Japan's asset bubble. Despite these setbacks, the market eventually recovered.
2. **September 11 Tragedy**: The markets fell significantly following the 9/11 attacks but have since risen to new highs over a 20-30 year span.

Speculating and Investing

Speculating involves taking on higher risk with the potential for high returns. While it may seem like gambling, when done in the right context, it can be profitable. Here are some speculative strategies:

1. **Mergers and Acquisitions**: Investing in companies involved in mergers or acquisitions can offer growth opportunities.

2. **Market Timing**: Trying to predict market movements can be risky but potentially rewarding for experienced investors.

However, even for speculators, diversification remains essential. Spreading investments across various opportunities can mitigate the risks associated with speculative ventures.

CHAPTER 18

Chapter 18: Building a Diversified Portfolio

Diversification is a crucial investment strategy that helps mitigate risk by spreading investments across various assets, sectors, and geographic regions. This chapter will guide you through the principles of diversification, asset allocation, and how to build a truly diversified portfolio.

Why Diversify?

The primary reason for diversification is to reduce risk. By spreading investments across different assets, you protect your portfolio from significant losses that could occur if a single investment or sector performs poorly. Diversification can help stabilize returns over time, providing a smoother investment journey.

Asset Allocation: The Key to Diversification

Asset allocation involves deciding how much of your money should be invested in different asset classes, such as stocks, bonds, and cash. The allocation is based on the risk and return characteristics of each asset class. Here's how to approach asset allocation:

1. **Determine Your Risk Tolerance**: Assess your risk tolerance, which is your ability and willingness to endure market fluctu-

ations. Younger investors typically have a higher risk tolerance, while those closer to retirement may prefer more stable investments.
2. **Set Investment Goals**: Define your investment goals, such as saving for retirement, buying a home, or funding education. Your goals will influence your asset allocation decisions.
3. **Choose Asset Classes**: Allocate your funds across different asset classes based on your risk tolerance and investment goals. For example:
    - **Stocks**: High risk, high return. Suitable for long-term growth.
    - **Bonds**: Lower risk, lower return. Provide income and stability.
    - **Cash**: Lowest risk, minimal return. Provides liquidity and safety.

Diversifying Within Asset Classes

Within each asset class, further diversify by investing in various sectors and regions. Here's an example of how to allocate a $100,000 investment:

1. **High-Risk Stocks**: Invest $30,000 in stocks from the banking sector. This sector offers high returns but comes with higher risk.
2. **Low-Risk Bonds**: Invest another $30,000 in utility bonds. Utilities are stable and provide steady returns, balancing the high-risk banking stocks.
3. **Other Sectors and Regions**: Allocate the remaining $40,000 across different sectors (e.g., technology, healthcare) and regions (e.g., international markets) to spread risk further.

Avoiding Common Pitfalls

Diversification is more complex than simply buying a variety of mutual funds or stocks. Here are common mistakes to avoid:

1. **Overconcentration**: Avoid putting too much money in one sector or asset class. Even if you own multiple stocks, if they are all in the same sector, your portfolio isn't truly diversified.
2. **Ignoring Correlation**: Investments that move in the same direction at the same time are highly correlated. Diversify across uncorrelated assets to reduce overall risk.
3. **Rebalancing**: Regularly review and adjust your portfolio to maintain your desired asset allocation. Market fluctuations can shift your allocations, increasing risk or reducing potential returns.

The Role of Index Funds

Index funds are an excellent tool for building a diversified portfolio, especially for beginners. Here's why:

1. **Broad Market Exposure**: Index funds replicate the performance of a market index, providing exposure to a wide range of stocks.
2. **Low Costs**: They typically have lower fees compared to actively managed funds, which helps maximize your returns.
3. **Simplicity**: Investing in index funds simplifies the diversification process, making it easier to achieve a balanced portfolio.

The Importance of Market Diversification

Market diversification involves spreading investments across different countries and industries. Here's how it helps:

1. **Geographic Diversification**: Investing in international markets reduces reliance on any single country's economy. This can provide stability during economic downturns in specific regions.
2. **Industry Diversification**: Spreading investments across various industries protects against sector-specific risks. For example, if the technology sector underperforms, investments in healthcare or consumer goods can offset losses.

CHAPTER 19

Chapter 19: Entrepreneurship and Business Ownershi

Entrepreneurship and business ownership represent a path to financial independence and personal fulfillment for many individuals. This chapter explores the various ways to make money, the potential of self-employment, and the journey of starting and growing your own business.

Infinite Ways to Make Money

There are countless avenues to generate income, including:

1. **Investing**: Stock market, real estate, bonds, and other financial instruments.
2. **Self-Employment**: Freelance work, consulting, and gig economy jobs.
3. **Business Ownership**: Starting and running your own business.

The Path to Ownership

Choosing to own a business is often considered the road less traveled, but it can lead to significant financial rewards. However, it requires careful planning, financial intelligence, and a willingness to take risks. Here are some key considerations:

1. **Financial Intelligence**: Understanding how to build credit, manage finances, and increase your credit score is crucial. Without this knowledge, an ambitious individual might jump into business ownership prematurely and face challenges.
2. **Freelance Work**: For those not yet ready for full business ownership, freelance work can be a great starting point. It provides flexibility, allows you to build skills and experience, and can be a stepping stone to starting your own business.

Personal Journey to Entrepreneurship

Reflecting on my personal journey, I had considered attending a trade college to become a barber before going to college. My friend encouraged me to pursue business ownership, and upon graduating, I recognized the potential of entrepreneurship. This path has become increasingly popular, as more people seek autonomy and financial independence. My parents, both business owners, further influenced my decision, as my experiences with corporate America reinforced my desire to work for myself.

The Entrepreneurial Mindset

To succeed in entrepreneurship, it's essential to cultivate the right mindset:

1. **Risk Tolerance**: Be prepared to take calculated risks. Business ownership involves uncertainty, but with proper planning and resilience, risks can be managed.
2. **Continuous Learning**: Stay informed about industry trends, business strategies, and financial management. Con-

tinuous learning is key to adapting and growing your business.
3. **Networking**: Build a strong network of mentors, peers, and industry contacts. Networking can provide support, opportunities, and valuable insights.

Steps to Starting a Business

Here's a roadmap to help you get started on your entrepreneurial journey:

1. **Idea Generation**: Identify a business idea that aligns with your interests, skills, and market demand. Conduct market research to validate your idea.
2. **Business Plan**: Create a detailed business plan outlining your vision, goals, target market, competitive analysis, and financial projections.
3. **Funding**: Determine how much capital you need and explore funding options, such as personal savings, loans, investors, or crowdfunding.
4. **Legal Structure**: Choose the appropriate legal structure for your business (e.g., sole proprietorship, partnership, LLC, corporation) and register your business.
5. **Branding and Marketing**: Develop your brand identity and marketing strategy to attract customers and build a strong online presence.
6. **Operations**: Set up your operations, including location, equipment, technology, and staffing. Ensure you have efficient processes in place.
7. **Launch**: Officially launch your business and start offering your products or services. Continuously monitor performance and adjust your strategies as needed.

Chapter 20: Passive Income Streams

Passive income is a desirable financial goal because it provides regular income with minimal ongoing effort. Understanding the different types of income and how to create passive income streams can help you achieve financial freedom and stability. This chapter will guide you through the basics of passive income, its benefits, and how to build your own passive income streams.

Understanding Income Types

There are three main categories of income: active income, residual income, and investment income.

1. **Active Income**: This is the most familiar type of income, earned through providing goods or services. It requires continuous effort to maintain, such as wages from a job or income from a business.
2. **Residual Income**: Similar to active income, but the effort to earn it has already been performed. Examples include royalties from a book or ongoing commissions. It provides more freedom and flexibility as the initial work continues to generate income.

3. **Investment Income**: This type of income comes from investments and typically starts generating returns long after the initial investment. Examples include dividends from stocks, interest from bonds, or rental income from real estate. High net worth individuals often use this income to build an estate for their descendants.

The Appeal of Passive Income

Passive income is particularly appealing because it offers financial security and the potential to significantly improve personal finances. Here's why it's so desirable:

1. **Financial Independence**: Passive income can reduce or eliminate the need to work for an employer, providing greater financial autonomy.
2. **Flexibility**: It offers the freedom to spend more time with family, pursue hobbies, or travel without the constraints of a traditional job.
3. **Risk Mitigation**: Diversifying income sources with passive streams can protect against financial instability if active income is disrupted.

Building Passive Income Streams

Creating passive income streams requires initial effort and investment, but the long-term benefits can be substantial. Here are some strategies to consider:

1. **Real Estate Investments**: Investing in rental properties can provide steady rental income. While it requires upfront capital and ongoing property management, real estate is a reliable source of passive income.

2. **Dividend Stocks**: Investing in dividend-paying stocks allows you to earn regular income through dividends. This requires a well-diversified portfolio and careful selection of reliable, high-yield stocks.
3. **Peer-to-Peer Lending**: Platforms that facilitate peer-to-peer lending allow you to earn interest by lending money to individuals or small businesses. This can provide attractive returns with manageable risk.
4. **Online Businesses**: E-commerce, affiliate marketing, and digital products (such as e-books or online courses) can generate passive income. While these businesses require initial setup and marketing, they can continue to produce income with minimal effort.
5. **Royalties and Licensing**: Creating intellectual property, such as books, music, or software, can generate ongoing royalties. Licensing agreements can also provide a steady stream of income from your creations.
6. **Automated Investments**: Robo-advisors and automated investment platforms can help you build a diversified portfolio that generates passive income through dividends, interest, and capital gains.

Steps to Create Passive Income

1. **Identify Opportunities**: Assess your skills, interests, and resources to identify suitable passive income opportunities. Choose methods that align with your strengths and financial goals.
2. **Initial Investment**: Be prepared to invest time, money, or both to set up your passive income streams. This could in-

clude purchasing real estate, creating digital products, or investing in stocks.
3. **Automate and Outsource**: Where possible, automate processes or outsource tasks to minimize ongoing effort. For example, hire a property manager for rental properties or use automated investment platforms.
4. **Monitor and Adjust**: Regularly review the performance of your passive income streams and make adjustments as needed to optimize returns.

CHAPTER 21

Chapter 21: Financial Education and Literacy

Financial education and literacy are fundamental to achieving and maintaining financial well-being. Understanding how to manage money effectively is a lifelong process that equips individuals with the knowledge, skills, and confidence to make informed financial decisions. This chapter explores the importance of financial education, the sources of financial literacy, and the role it plays in building wealth and achieving financial freedom.

The Importance of Financial Education

Financial education is the formal process through which individuals learn to obtain and manage money. It encompasses a wide range of topics, including budgeting, saving, investing, credit management, and retirement planning. The importance of financial education cannot be overstated, as it lays the groundwork for sound financial decision-making throughout life.

Sources of Financial Literacy

Financial literacy can be acquired from various sources, each contributing to an individual's understanding of money management:

1. **Parents and Family**: Financial habits and attitudes often start at home. Parents and family members can impart valuable lessons about saving, spending, and investing.
2. **Schools and Educational Institutions**: Many schools now incorporate financial education into their curricula, teaching students the basics of personal finance.
3. **Media**: Newspapers, magazines, television programs, and online resources offer a wealth of information on financial topics.
4. **Financial Services Industry**: Banks, credit unions, and financial advisors provide resources and guidance to help individuals manage their finances.
5. **Life Experiences**: Personal experiences, both positive and negative, contribute to an individual's financial literacy. Learning from mistakes and successes is crucial for financial growth.

The Lifelong Process of Financial Literacy

Financial literacy is not a one-time achievement but a continuous journey. It involves adapting to changing financial circumstances and needs, staying informed about financial products and services, and being proactive in managing money. A financially literate individual can navigate various financial challenges and opportunities without relying heavily on others for help.

Achieving Financial Freedom: A Marathon, Not a Sprint

Achieving financial freedom is a long-term goal that requires patience, discipline, and perseverance. It involves several key steps:

1. **Paying Down Debt**: Reducing and eventually eliminating debt is a critical component of financial freedom. It frees up resources for saving and investing.

2. **Saving Money**: Building an emergency fund and saving for future goals are essential for financial stability.
3. **Investing Wisely**: Investing in a diversified portfolio of assets helps grow wealth over time and provides financial security.

The Role of Financial Education in Wealth Building

Financial education and literacy are cornerstones for building wealth. They enable individuals to make informed decisions, avoid common financial pitfalls, and seize opportunities for growth. Here's how financial literacy contributes to wealth building:

1. **Informed Decision-Making**: Understanding financial concepts and products allows individuals to make better choices about spending, saving, and investing.
2. **Risk Management**: Financial literacy helps individuals assess and manage risks, such as those associated with investments and debt.
3. **Opportunity Recognition**: A well-informed person can identify and capitalize on financial opportunities that others might overlook.

Learning from Mistakes

The path to financial freedom is often filled with challenges and setbacks. Mistakes are inevitable, but they provide valuable learning experiences. Financially astute individuals use these experiences to improve their financial strategies and better prepare for future challenges.

CHAPTER 22

Chapter 22: Mindset and Psychology of Wealth

The mindset and psychology of wealth are deeply rooted in the family unit and the experiences one has growing up. These early lessons and attitudes about money can have a profound impact on one's financial behavior and decisions throughout life. This chapter explores how these influences shape our financial mindset and how we can consciously change our financial position.

Inheritance and Family Influence

The cycle of wealth often begins with inheritance and the family unit. The financial lessons imparted by parents and family members play a crucial role in shaping our attitudes toward money. Consider these reflective questions:

- **What were you taught about money by your parents?**
- **What is your earliest memory involving money?**
- **What did your parents teach you about your financial future?**
- **Do they still provide you with financial assistance?**
- **What is your attitude about providing the same financial assistance to your children?**

The answers to these questions reveal how family influences, regardless of socio-economic status, shape our financial behaviors and attitudes.

The Impact of Economic Conditions

Each generation's attitude towards money is often influenced by the economic conditions they experience. For example:

- **Children of The Great Depression**: Those who grew up during the Great Depression often developed a strong habit of saving, fearing the return of hard times. This experience made them more risk-averse and focused on financial security.
- **Boomers and Millennials**: Boomers, having experienced post-war economic growth, may have a different outlook compared to Millennials, who faced the Great Recession and significant student loan debt.

These experiences contribute to the family's financial position and prosperity relative to the broader economic context of their time.

Breaking the Cycle

While family influences and economic conditions shape our financial mindset, it's important to remember that we have the power to change our financial position. Here are some steps to take control of your financial future:

1. **Self-Awareness**: Recognize the financial habits and attitudes you inherited from your family. Understanding these influences is the first step towards making conscious changes.
2. **Education**: Educate yourself about personal finance through books, courses, and professional advice. Knowledge is a powerful tool for transforming your financial mindset.

3. **Goal Setting**: Set clear financial goals and create a plan to achieve them. Whether it's saving for a home, paying off debt, or investing for retirement, having specific goals helps guide your financial decisions.
4. **Positive Habits**: Develop positive financial habits, such as budgeting, saving, and investing. Consistency in these habits can lead to long-term financial success.
5. **Mindset Shift**: Cultivate a growth mindset towards money. Believe in your ability to improve your financial situation through smart decisions and hard work.

Teaching the Next Generation

As you work on improving your financial mindset, consider how you can positively influence the next generation. Here are some tips for teaching children about money:

1. **Early Education**: Start teaching children about money from a young age. Use everyday activities, such as shopping or saving for a toy, as teachable moments.
2. **Lead by Example**: Demonstrate good financial habits. Children often learn by observing their parents' behavior.
3. **Encourage Saving and Giving**: Teach children the importance of saving and giving. Help them set up a savings account and involve them in charitable activities.
4. **Open Discussions**: Have open and honest discussions about money. Encourage questions and provide clear, age-appropriate answers.

CHAPTER 23

Chapter 23: Success Stories and Case Studies

The topic of student loans often feels dark and hopeless for many students, who perceive their financial future as being overshadowed by debt. However, hearing firsthand experiences from others who have successfully overcome similar challenges can provide inspiration and practical insights. This chapter shares real-life success stories and case studies of individuals who have won the battle against student loans.

Andrew and His Wife's Journey to Debt Freedom

Andrew and his wife faced a daunting combined student loan debt of $70,000. When they calculated the payoff date at their current payment pace, it was going to take them 28 years to become debt-free. Initially, Andrew felt overwhelmed and considered resigning to a life of debt. However, a co-worker informed him about a loan repayment program that would increase their minimum payment to cover the interest and a bit more.

Though it was tough at first, they committed to the program and eventually doubled their minimum payments. The quick progress they saw motivated them to set and stick to a goal of paying off the loan in five years. They quickly cut frivolous spending, decreased entertainment expenses, and almost never went out to eat. With determination and discipline, they paid off the loans in just three years. Andrew reflects, "To this day, I do not know how we did it. It was tough at times, but it feels so good to be done, and it's a lesson that will stay with us for the rest of our lives."

More Success Stories

To further inspire students, here are two additional examples of individuals who have successfully navigated their way out of student loan debt:

1. **Emma's Strategic Savings and Extra Income Efforts**:
    - **Situation**: Emma graduated with $50,000 in student loan debt. With a modest salary, she realized it would take decades to pay off the debt if she only made minimum payments.
    - **Strategy**: Emma created a strict budget, cutting non-essential expenses and focusing on necessities. She also took on freelance writing gigs to earn extra income.
    - **Outcome**: Through diligent savings and additional income, Emma managed to pay off her loans in six years. She now shares her story to motivate others in similar situations.
2. **Michael's Side Hustle Success**:
    - **Situation**: Michael had $80,000 in student loan debt and felt trapped by the financial burden. Determined to pay it off quickly, he explored various side hustle opportunities.
    - **Strategy**: Michael started a successful online business selling handmade crafts. He devoted evenings and weekends to growing his business, while still working his full-time job.

- **Outcome**: Michael's side hustle significantly boosted his income, allowing him to pay off his student loans in five years. His story demonstrates the power of creativity and hard work in overcoming financial challenges.

Lessons from Success Stories

These success stories highlight several key lessons for managing and eliminating student loan debt:

1. **Commitment and Discipline**: Sticking to a repayment plan and making sacrifices in spending habits are crucial for achieving debt freedom.
2. **Exploring Repayment Options**: Investigating different loan repayment programs can provide more manageable solutions.
3. **Generating Additional Income**: Side hustles and freelance work can significantly accelerate debt repayment.
4. **Sharing Experiences**: Hearing success stories from others can provide motivation and practical strategies for managing debt.

CHAPTER 24

Chapter 24: Financial Mistakes to Avoid

Building wealth and achieving financial freedom requires not only smart financial planning and disciplined saving but also the avoidance of common financial pitfalls. These mistakes can undermine your hard work and set back your progress. This chapter will highlight key financial mistakes to avoid and provide practical advice to help you stay on track.

Prioritize Family and Personal Relationships

Your financial decisions should support, not undermine, your personal and family relationships. Focus on what truly matters rather than on impressing others with material possessions. Here's why:

1. **Financial Soundness**: Buying necessities with cash and avoiding unnecessary luxuries until you can afford them is the most financially sound approach. It leads to a more disciplined and enjoyable life.
2. **Long-Term Happiness**: True happiness comes from meaningful relationships and experiences, not from owning flashy items.

Avoid Living Above Your Means

One of the most critical mistakes to avoid is living above your means. A high consumption lifestyle can quickly deplete your hard-earned money. Here's how to steer clear of this trap:

1. **Recognize the Social Norms**: In America, there's a societal pressure to own big houses, flashy cars, boats, clothes, and jewelry. This phenomenon, known as "keeping up with the Joneses," can lead to financial ruin.
2. **Understand the Costs**: Financing luxury items often comes with high costs and even higher maintenance expenses. These purchases provide only temporary pleasure and can leave you in deeper debt.
3. **Practical Approach**: Focus on buying what you need and can afford. This approach prevents financial strain and fosters a healthier financial lifestyle.

Common Financial Mistakes

To build wealth and achieve a debt-free life, it's important to be aware of and avoid these common financial mistakes:

1. **Not Having a Budget**: Without a budget, it's easy to overspend and lose track of your financial goals. Create a budget and stick to it to manage your money effectively.
2. **Failing to Save for Emergencies**: Not having an emergency fund can lead to financial crises when unexpected expenses arise. Aim to save at least three to six months' worth of living expenses.
3. **Relying on Credit Cards**: Using credit cards for everyday purchases can lead to high-interest debt. Pay off your credit card balance in full each month to avoid interest charges.

4. **Not Investing**: Avoiding investments out of fear or lack of knowledge can hinder wealth building. Educate yourself about different investment options and start investing early.
5. **Ignoring Retirement Planning**: Failing to plan for retirement can result in financial difficulties in later life. Contribute regularly to retirement accounts and take advantage of employer matching programs.
6. **Making Emotional Financial Decisions**: Financial decisions driven by emotions, such as panic selling during market downturns, can lead to losses. Stay calm and stick to your financial plan.

Remaining Mindful

The challenge in avoiding these mistakes lies in staying mindful about your financial decisions. Here are some tips to help you stay on track:

1. **Educate Yourself**: Continuously educate yourself about personal finance and stay informed about best practices.
2. **Seek Advice**: Consult financial advisors or mentors for guidance and support.
3. **Review Your Goals**: Regularly review your financial goals and adjust your strategies as needed.
4. **Practice Self-Discipline**: Develop and maintain self-discipline in your spending and saving habits.

By avoiding these common financial mistakes and remaining mindful of your financial decisions, you can build a solid foundation for wealth and achieve financial freedom.

Chapter 25: Strategies for Long-Term Wealth Preser

Preserving wealth over the long term requires careful planning, continuous monitoring, and periodic adjustments to your investment strategy. This chapter will guide you through the essential strategies for ensuring your wealth remains intact and grows steadily over time.

Monitoring and Reassessment

One of the key components of long-term wealth preservation is regularly monitoring your investment's progress and reassessing the suitability of your strategy. Here's how to stay on track:

1. **Regular Reviews**: Periodically review your investment portfolio to assess its performance and alignment with your goals. This helps identify any necessary adjustments due to changes in your investment time frame, capital, or financial needs.
2. **Adjust for Changes**: Make adjustments to your investment allocation whenever there are significant changes in your life circumstances or the investment environment.

Rebalancing the Portfolio

Rebalancing is a crucial process for maintaining your original asset allocation and managing risk. Here's why and how to rebalance effectively:

1. **Buy Low, Sell High**: Rebalancing involves selling assets that have performed well and buying assets that have underperformed. This contrarian investing approach forces you to buy low and sell high.
2. **Manage Costs**: Although rebalancing incurs transaction costs, studies show that it improves the risk and return characteristics of a portfolio, justifying the expense.
3. **Example**: During the Global Financial Crisis (GFC), rebalancing would have involved selling expensive bonds and buying cheaper equities to maintain the desired asset allocation.

Accumulation and Income Phases

Your investment strategy should evolve as you transition from the accumulation phase to the income phase. Here's how to navigate these stages:

1. **Accumulation Phase**: Focus on investing for income and growth. Since income is generally less than future needs, capital is accumulated to fund those future needs.
2. **Income Phase**: As you approach retirement or need regular income from your investments, capital preservation becomes more important. Shift to a more conservative investment strategy to reduce exposure to growth assets and avoid excessive risk.

Developing a Financial Plan

A comprehensive financial plan is essential for long-term wealth preservation. Here's what your plan should include:

1. **Diversified Investment Allocation**: Spread your investments across various asset classes to balance risk and return.
2. **Projected Future Required Capital**: Estimate the capital needed to meet your future financial goals.
3. **Contingency Reserves**: Set aside reserves to cover unexpected expenses or market downturns.

Asset Allocation

Asset allocation is a significant determinant of portfolio returns. Here are some strategies:

1. **Risk and Return Trade-Off**: Make choices based on your risk tolerance and return expectations. For example, a high-risk, high-return strategy might allocate 70% to equities and 30% to secure assets like bonds or cash.
2. **Income from Dividends**: Investing in dividend-paying stocks can provide a steady income stream and help preserve capital.
3. **Tax Efficiency**: Consider tax-efficient investments, such as Australian shares for retirees who often fall into a lower income tax bracket.

Capital Preservation Strategies

Capital preservation becomes increasingly important as you transition to drawing income from your investments. Here's how to focus on preserving your capital:

1. **Conservative Allocation**: Shift to a more conservative investment allocation, reducing exposure to high-risk growth assets.
2. **Income-Producing Investments**: Focus on investments that provide reliable income, such as bonds, dividend-paying stocks, and real estate.
3. **Risk Management**: Implement strategies to protect your capital from market volatility and economic downturns.

CHAPTER 26

Chapter 26: Philanthropy and Giving Back

Philanthropy is often seen as the domain of the mega-wealthy, but even those in the wealth-building phase can incorporate giving back into their financial plan. By developing a habit of regular, small contributions, you can make a significant impact over time while fostering a positive attitude towards wealth and charity. This chapter will explore how to start giving back, the benefits of philanthropy, and practical strategies for effective charitable giving.

Starting with Small Contributions

Incorporating philanthropy into your financial plan doesn't require vast amounts of money. Here's how you can start with small, manageable steps:

1. **Set Aside a Small Percentage**: Begin by setting aside a small, regular portion of your income for charity. As little as two percent of your yearly income can accumulate into a significant sum over time.
2. **Develop a Habit**: Making regular contributions will habituate positive giving behavior. Over time, this practice will become a natural and rewarding part of your financial routine.

3. **Mitigate Loss of Capital**: The small loss of capital from charitable donations is often offset by the personal satisfaction and sense of purpose gained from supporting meaningful causes.

Avoiding Impulsive Giving

To ensure your charitable contributions have the most impact, it's important to avoid impulsive and unfocused giving. Here are some tips:

1. **Set Specific Goals**: Define clear goals for your charitable giving. Decide which causes you want to support and how much you plan to donate.
2. **Research Charities**: Conduct thorough research to find reputable charities that align with your values. Look for organizations with a track record of effectively using donations to achieve their goals.
3. **Beware of Telemarketing**: Be cautious of donation requests and telemarketing campaigns. Stick to your planned giving strategy to avoid being swayed by emotional appeals.

The Broader Impact of Philanthropy

Now that you've worked hard to build your wealth, it's time to consider how you can use it to benefit others. Philanthropy offers numerous benefits beyond the financial:

1. **Helping Others**: Philanthropy is the practice of helping others through donations of money, time, or skills. It directly improves the quality of life for those in need.

2. **Personal Satisfaction**: Giving back provides a deep sense of personal satisfaction and connection to the community. It's a way to invest in a better world for future generations.
3. **Creating Positive Change**: Philanthropic efforts contribute to social change and can leave a lasting legacy. By supporting causes you care about, you help create a more equitable and compassionate society.

Treating Philanthropy as an Investment

Approach philanthropy with the same strategic mindset as you would with financial investments:

1. **Conduct Research**: Just as with financial investments, research is crucial. Identify where your funds are needed most and what kind of impact they can make.
2. **Target Your Funds**: Focus your donations on areas where they will have the greatest effect. This ensures your contributions are used efficiently and effectively.
3. **Measure Impact**: Consider the return on investment (ROI) of your philanthropic efforts. Evaluate the tangible benefits your donations provide to the recipients and the broader community.

Ways to Give Back

There are many ways to practice philanthropy, each offering different opportunities to make a positive impact:

1. **Monetary Donations**: Contributing money to charities and non-profit organizations is the most direct way to support causes you care about.

2. **Volunteering Time**: Donating your time and skills can be equally valuable. Volunteering provides hands-on support and helps you connect with the community.
3. **In-Kind Donations**: Donating goods and services can meet immediate needs and provide crucial resources to those in need.
4. **Creating Foundations**: For those with significant wealth, establishing a charitable foundation allows for structured and sustained giving over time.

CHAPTER 27

Chapter 27: Financial Independence and Early Retir

The goal of financial independence and early retirement is to reach a point where you no longer need to work to sustain your lifestyle. This chapter explores the importance of entrepreneurship, the need to understand your financial requirements post-retirement, and the steps required to achieve financial independence.

The Role of Entrepreneurship

Achieving financial independence often means moving beyond a traditional salary. Here's why entrepreneurship plays a crucial role:

1. **Limitations of a Salary**: While high-paying jobs such as those held by doctors, lawyers, and accountants provide substantial income, they often tie earnings to the time worked. If they stop working, the income stops as well. This situation is akin to taking a vacation rather than true retirement.
2. **Revenue Streams**: Entrepreneurship allows you to create multiple revenue streams, decoupling your earnings from the time you put in. This means you can continue to earn money

even when you're not actively working, paving the way for true financial independence.

Calculating Retirement Needs

To plan for financial independence and early retirement, it's essential to understand your financial needs post-retirement:

1. **Estimate Expenses**: Consider how much money you will need to live on once you stop earning a salary. While your first instinct might be to aim for 100% of your pre-retirement income, this might not be necessary. Factors to consider include:
    - **Retirement Fund Contributions**: You will no longer need to contribute to your retirement fund.
    - **Paid Off Mortgage**: You may have paid off your mortgage, reducing your expenses.
    - **Independent Children**: Your children may be financially independent.
    - **Lower Taxes**: If your income is lower, your income taxes will be lower as well.
2. **Adjust for Inflation**: Calculate a reasonable annual expenditure and adjust for inflation. Compare this amount to your projected investment income to assess whether your investments can support your spending needs.
3. **Build Wealth Aggressively**: If your investment income falls short, consider strategies to aggressively build your wealth. Conversely, if you're in good shape, you may choose to ease up and avoid unnecessary saving.

Steps to Financial Independence

Financial independence is a long-term journey that requires careful planning and disciplined execution. Here are the steps to guide you towards this goal:

1. **Set Clear Goals**: Define your financial independence and early retirement goals. Determine how much money you need to save and invest to reach your desired lifestyle.
2. **Create a Financial Plan**: Develop a comprehensive financial plan that includes budgeting, saving, investing, and risk management strategies. Ensure your plan aligns with your goals and timelines.
3. **Increase Income Streams**: Explore ways to increase your income, such as starting a side business, investing in real estate, or creating passive income streams. Diversifying your income sources reduces reliance on a single stream.
4. **Live Below Your Means**: Practice frugality and discipline in your spending. Living below your means allows you to save and invest more, accelerating your journey to financial independence.
5. **Invest Wisely**: Focus on long-term investments that provide growth and income. Diversify your portfolio to manage risk and optimize returns.
6. **Regularly Review and Adjust**: Monitor your progress and make adjustments as needed. Rebalance your investment portfolio, reassess your goals, and stay informed about financial trends.
7. **Stay Committed**: Achieving financial independence requires patience, discipline, and persistence. Stay committed to your plan and adapt as necessary to stay on track.

CHAPTER 28

Chapter 28: Financial Planning for Different Life

Financial planning is a dynamic process that evolves with each stage of life. Understanding the unique financial challenges and opportunities at different life stages is crucial for effective wealth building and debt management. This chapter explores the financial planning strategies for various life stages, including married couples, single individuals, single parents, and dual-income families.

Financial Planning for Married Couples
Married Couples with No Children:

1. **Economic Security**: Married couples without children require a slightly higher level of economic security compared to single individuals. They may take on debt, such as a mortgage, to improve their standard of living.
2. **Debt Management**: Effective debt management is crucial. Couples should focus on managing and reducing debt to build a strong financial foundation.

Married Couples with Children:

1. **Increased Financial Needs**: With children, the level of economic security required increases. Additional expenses include childcare, education, and healthcare.
2. **Wealth Building**: High-income dual-earner families have significant wealth-building potential but must be cautious of misusing income on high living. Prioritize savings and investments to secure the family's financial future.

Financial Planning for Single Individuals
Single People:

1. **Lower Economic Security Requirement**: Single individuals generally have fewer dependents and lower financial needs.
2. **Savings and Investment**: Focus on building savings and investing for future goals. Single individuals have more flexibility to take on higher-risk investments for potential higher returns.

Single Parents:

1. **Economic Security**: Single parents often have financial needs similar to married couples with the same number of dependents. They face the challenge of supporting a household on a single income.
2. **Debt Management**: Managing debt is critical. Single parents should prioritize paying down high-interest debt and building an emergency fund to ensure financial stability.
3. **Budgeting**: Create a strict budget to manage expenses and ensure all financial needs are met.

Financial Planning for Different Income Households

Single-Income Households:

1. **Challenges**: Single-income households may struggle with debt and living expenses. Effective financial planning can help improve economic security.
2. **Strategic Savings**: Focus on saving and investing to build a financial cushion. This can help manage unexpected expenses and reduce reliance on credit.

Dual-Income Households:

1. **Wealth-Building Potential**: Dual-income families often have higher wealth-building potential. However, they must avoid the trap of high consumption lifestyles that can deplete savings.
2. **Debt Management**: Prioritize paying off high-interest debt and avoid taking on new debt unnecessarily. This ensures a more secure financial future.

Aggressive Debt Repayment Strategies

Effective debt management is a precursor to successful financial planning. Here are strategies to aggressively pay down debt:

1. **Debt Snowball Method**: Focus on paying off the smallest debt first while making minimum payments on larger debts. This builds momentum and provides psychological motivation.
2. **Debt Avalanche Method**: Prioritize paying off the debt with the highest interest rate first. This saves money on interest over time and reduces overall debt more efficiently.

3. **Consolidation and Refinancing**: Consider consolidating high-interest debts into a single lower-interest loan. Refinancing can also lower interest rates and reduce monthly payments.

Preparing for Different Life Stages

Financial planning should adapt to changes in financial stability and household size. Here's how to prepare for different life stages:

1. **Life Transitions**: Anticipate major life changes, such as marriage, children, or career changes. Adjust your financial plan to accommodate these changes.
2. **Emergency Fund**: Maintain an emergency fund to cover unexpected expenses. Aim for at least three to six months' worth of living expenses.
3. **Investment Strategy**: Adjust your investment strategy based on your life stage and risk tolerance. Younger individuals can take on more risk, while older individuals should focus on preserving capital.

By implementing effective financial planning and debt management strategies, you can build and preserve wealth, ensuring economic security at every stage of life.

CHAPTER 29

Chapter 29: Navigating Economic Challenges

Navigating economic challenges requires a deep understanding of economic principles and a keen awareness of current economic conditions. Economic illiteracy is rampant today, leading to misunderstandings and poor financial decisions. This chapter explores the complexities of the economy, the impact of economic downturns, and strategies to safeguard your wealth during challenging times.

Understanding Economics

Economics is not an act of nature, but an act of men. The economic problems we face often have solutions, but these solutions can be designed to benefit specific interests. Here's why understanding economics is crucial:

1. **Informed Decisions**: Without a solid understanding of economics, making safe and effective financial decisions is challenging. Knowledge of economic principles helps you navigate financial complexities and avoid common pitfalls.
2. **Complexity of Recessions**: Recessions are often misunderstood as natural cycles. In reality, they are complex events in-

fluenced by human actions and decisions. Understanding the underlying causes of economic downturns is key to making informed decisions.

The Impact of Economic Downturns

An economic downturn or recession is characterized by a decline in general economic activity. Here's how it affects businesses and consumers:

1. **Reduction in Real Income**: Economic downturns often result in decreased real income, reducing purchasing power.
2. **Increased Unemployment**: Job losses rise, leading to higher unemployment rates and financial instability for many families.
3. **Slowing Industrial Capacity**: Industrial and economic capacity slows down, impacting production and economic growth.
4. **Consumer Fear**: Fear of economic instability leads consumers to cut back on spending, further slowing the economy.

Implementing Debt-Free Strategies

During economic downturns, it's crucial to implement debt-free strategies to maintain financial stability. Here's why and how:

1. **Avoiding Increased Debt**: Taking on more debt during a recession can lead to financial insecurity. Instead, focus on reducing existing debt and avoiding new debt.
2. **Economic Capacity**: Borrowing should be considered when the economic capacity is increasing, not during downturns. Understanding current economic conditions helps you make prudent borrowing decisions.

Understanding Current Economic Conditions

To make wise financial decisions, you need to understand current economic conditions. Here's how to stay informed:

1. **Economic Indicators**: Pay attention to economic indicators such as GDP growth, unemployment rates, inflation, and consumer confidence. These indicators provide insights into the health of the economy.
2. **Financial News**: Follow reputable financial news sources to stay updated on economic trends and developments.
3. **Government Reports**: Review government reports and publications on economic policy and performance. These can provide valuable context for understanding economic conditions.

Strategies for Safeguarding Wealth

Here are practical strategies to safeguard your wealth during economic challenges:

1. **Diversify Investments**: Spread your investments across different asset classes to reduce risk. Diversification helps protect your portfolio from significant losses in any one sector.
2. **Maintain an Emergency Fund**: Ensure you have an emergency fund to cover at least three to six months' worth of living expenses. This provides a financial cushion during periods of economic uncertainty.
3. **Reduce Debt**: Focus on paying down high-interest debt to improve your financial stability. Avoid taking on new debt during economic downturns.

4. **Budget and Save**: Create a strict budget to manage your expenses and increase savings. Cutting unnecessary spending helps build a financial buffer.
5. **Stay Informed**: Continuously educate yourself about economic conditions and financial strategies. Knowledge empowers you to make informed decisions and adapt to changing circumstances.

Chapter 30: Balancing Work and Life

Achieving a balance between work and life is a dynamic process, not a fixed state. It involves finding an acceptable rhythm between periods of intense work and time spent on life maintenance and recreation. This chapter explores how to maintain a healthy work-life balance, avoid common pitfalls, and create a fulfilling life.

The Dynamic Nature of Work-Life Balance

Balancing work and life requires ongoing adjustments as your career and personal circumstances evolve. Here's how to navigate this balance:

1. **Intense Work Periods**: There will be times when you need to work long, hard hours. During these periods, it's crucial to maintain substantial healthy recreation or life maintenance activities to ensure a good quality of life.
2. **Preventing Build-Up**: Avoid letting life activities accumulate to the point where they become overwhelming. Managing these activities regularly prevents them from turning into additional work.

Avoiding Common Mistakes

A common mistake is allowing too much leisure and recreation time during periods of reduced income or unemployment. Here's why this can be problematic:

1. **Temporary Relief**: While indulging in leisure activities may provide temporary relief, it is not sustainable in the long run and can lead to further feelings of time and income pressure.
2. **Balanced Approach**: It's essential to strike a balance between leisure and productive activities, even during times of reduced income. This helps maintain financial stability and personal well-being.

Identifying Meaningful Activities

To achieve a balanced work-life rhythm, it's important to identify activities that genuinely contribute to your well-being:

1. **Healthy Recreation**: Engage in activities that promote physical and mental health, such as exercise, hobbies, and spending time with loved ones.
2. **Avoid Passive Activities**: Distinguish between activities that genuinely make you feel good and passive activities or consumptive buying that may provide short-term pleasure but not long-term satisfaction.
3. **Simpler Life**: Embrace a simpler life with meaningful activities that cost less and can be sustained even during periods of less income or financial security.

Reducing Clutter and Enhancing Quality

If you find that life maintenance activities require too much time and money, it may be time to reassess and reduce clutter:

1. **Assess Activities**: Evaluate which activities add real quality to your life and which ones are merely adding to the workload without significant benefits.
2. **Streamline Life Maintenance**: Simplify life maintenance activities to focus on what truly matters. This can free up time and resources for more fulfilling pursuits.

Practical Steps to Balance Work and Life

Here are some practical steps to help you balance work and life effectively:

1. **Set Boundaries**: Establish clear boundaries between work and personal life. This includes setting specific work hours and ensuring you have time for relaxation and recreation.
2. **Prioritize Tasks**: Identify your most important tasks and focus on completing them. Prioritizing helps manage time effectively and reduces stress.
3. **Schedule Downtime**: Plan regular downtime to recharge and engage in activities you enjoy. This helps prevent burnout and maintains overall well-being.
4. **Practice Self-Care**: Incorporate self-care routines into your daily life. This can include exercise, meditation, reading, or any activity that promotes mental and physical health.
5. **Seek Support**: Don't hesitate to seek support from family, friends, or professionals. Building a support system can help you navigate challenges and maintain balance.

Conclusion

Balancing work and life is an ongoing process that requires awareness, intention, and flexibility. By identifying meaningful activities, avoiding common pitfalls, and simplifying life maintenance, you can create a fulfilling and balanced life. Remember, it's not about achieving a perfect state but finding a rhythm that works for you.

CHAPTER 31

Chapter 31: Resources and Tools

In the journey to building wealth and achieving financial independence, having the right resources and tools is crucial. This chapter focuses on where to seek advice, the importance of continued education, and the best strategies for utilizing financial resources effectively.

Seeking Advice from Successful People

To make informed financial decisions, seek advice from those who have strong knowledge and experience in investing and wealth building. Here's how to find and leverage the right advisors:

1. **Identify Knowledgeable Individuals**: Look for professionals, online mentors, friends, or family members who are knowledgeable about finance. Ensure they have a track record of success and practice what they preach.
2. **Diverse Opinions**: Always get a second or third opinion. Not everyone with a high income is wealthy or provides sound advice. Multiple perspectives can provide a more balanced view.

3. **Mentorship**: Find someone who has achieved the financial goals you aspire to. A mentor can offer guidance, share their experiences, and help you avoid common pitfalls.

Continuing Financial Education

Ongoing education is critical for understanding wealth-building strategies and managing debt. Here's why and how to keep educating yourself:

1. **Wealth-Building Strategies**: Understanding different strategies for building wealth is essential. This includes investments, savings, budgeting, and debt management.
2. **Impact of Debt**: Learn how debt can impact your ability to build wealth. Understanding when and how to use debt responsibly is crucial.
3. **Workshops and Seminars**: Attend workshops and seminars on investing, personal finance, and debt management regularly. Repeated exposure to financial concepts reinforces learning and helps retain information.
4. **Online Resources**: Utilize online courses, webinars, and financial blogs. These resources can provide up-to-date information and practical tips.

Utilizing Financial Resources Effectively

Using the right tools and resources can make a significant difference in your financial journey. Here are some key resources and strategies:

1. **Financial Planning Software**: Use financial planning software to track your income, expenses, investments, and progress towards financial goals. Tools like Mint, Personal

Capital, and YNAB (You Need a Budget) can help manage your finances effectively.
2. **Investment Platforms**: Explore investment platforms like Robinhood, E*TRADE, or Vanguard to invest in stocks, bonds, and other assets. These platforms offer various tools to help you make informed investment decisions.
3. **Books and Literature**: Read books on personal finance and investing. Classics like "Rich Dad Poor Dad" by Robert Kiyosaki, "The Intelligent Investor" by Benjamin Graham, and "Your Money or Your Life" by Vicki Robin provide valuable insights.
4. **Financial Advisors**: Consider hiring a certified financial advisor for personalized advice. Advisors can help create a tailored financial plan and provide ongoing support.

Debt Management Tools

Managing debt is a crucial aspect of financial planning. Here are some tools and strategies to help you manage debt effectively:

1. **Debt Repayment Calculators**: Use online calculators to create a debt repayment plan. These tools can help you understand how long it will take to pay off your debt and the total interest you'll pay.
2. **Debt Consolidation**: Explore options for consolidating high-interest debts into a single, lower-interest loan. This can simplify repayments and reduce overall interest costs.
3. **Credit Counseling**: Seek credit counseling services if you're struggling with debt. Counselors can provide advice, negotiate with creditors, and help you create a debt management plan.

4. **Automatic Payments**: Set up automatic payments to ensure you never miss a due date. This helps avoid late fees and keeps your credit score healthy.

CHAPTER 32

Chapter 32: Conclusion

Have you had enough yet? The journey to becoming and remaining debt-free is undoubtedly challenging, but it stands among the most worthwhile endeavors you can undertake. It requires a lifetime commitment and a fundamental change in mindset.

To rid yourself of debt, you must begin to think differently. Imagine the quality of life you can achieve by becoming debt-free and building wealth. The benefits of acquiring wealth are worth the sacrifices along the way.

Here are some key takeaways:

1. **Commitment to Change**: Becoming debt-free requires a commitment to changing your spending and saving habits. It's about making conscious, informed decisions every day.
2. **Building Wealth**: Devote the extra income you'll have from being debt-free to building wealth. This means investing wisely and creating a safety net for the future.
3. **Financial Freedom**: Achieving financial freedom means having enough investment income to support your cost of living. Practice wise spending now to reap the benefits of your efforts later.

4. **Life Without Debt**: Once you've achieved financial freedom, you'll no longer worry about being debt-ridden. This peace of mind is invaluable and worth striving for.

Remember, the road to financial freedom is not a sprint but a marathon. Stay disciplined, keep educating yourself, and make smart financial decisions. Your future self will thank you.

Isn't that worth a try?

Milton Keynes UK
Ingram Content Group UK Ltd.
UKHW031115261124
451585UK00004B/527